A PLACE IN HISTORY

HIROSHIMA

...I said, "Yeah, we're going on a bombing mission, but it's a little bit special." My tailgunner, Bob Caron, was pretty alert. He said, "Colonel, we wouldn't be playing with atoms today, would we?" I said, "Bob, you've got it just exactly right." So I went back and told the [others]. I said, "OK, this is an atom bomb we're dropping" ... I didn't see any change in their faces or anything else.

Colonel Paul Tibbets recalls talking to his crew shortly after takeoff. From an interview with Studs Terkel, 2002.

A PLACE IN HISTORY

HIROSHIMA

STEWART ROSS

ARCTURUS

Reprinted in 2012
This edition first published in 2010 by Arcturus Publishing
Distributed by Black Rabbit Books
P.O. Box 3263
Mankato
Minnesota MN 56002

Printed in the United States

The right of Stewart Ross to be identified as the author of this
work has been asserted by him in accordance with the
Copyright, Designs and Patents Act 1988.

Series concept: Alex Woolf
Editors: Sean Connolly and Alex Woolf
Designer: Phipps Design
Picture research: Alex Woolf
Map illustrator: Stefan Chabluk

Library of Congress Cataloging-in-Publication Data

Ross, Stewart.
  Hiroshima / Stewart Ross.
    p. cm. -- (A place in history)
  Includes bibliographical references and index.
  ISBN 978-1-84837-674-8 (library binding)
  1. Hiroshima-shi (Japan)--History--Bombardment, 1945--
Juvenile literature. 2. Atomic bomb--Japan--Hiroshima-shi--
History--Juvenile literature. I. Title.
  D767.25.H6R67 2011
  940.54'2521954--dc22
              2010014149

Picture Credits
Arcturus: 9 (Stefan Chabluk).
Corbis: cover *foreground* (Bettmann), cover *background* (John van
Hasselt/Sygma), 6–7 (John van Hasselt/Sygma), 11 (Bettmann), 13
(Hulton-Deutsch Collection), 15 (Bettmann), 16 (Bettmann), 17 (Philip
Gendreau), 19 (Bettmann), 20 (Bettmann), 21 (Bettmann), 22
(Bettmann), 23, 24 (Walter Bibikow), 25 (Karen Kasmauski), 26
(Bettmann), 27 (Bettmann), 28 (Louie Psihoyos/Science Faction), 29
(Bettmann), 30 (Bettmann), 31 (Bettmann), 32 (Bettmann), 33
(Hulton-Deutsch Collection), 35 (Bettmann), 36 (Bettmann), 37
(Bettmann), 39 (Jo Yong-Hak/Reuters), 40 (Bettmann), 41 (Shen Hong/
XinHua/Xinhua Press), 42 (Sen/Amana Images), 43 (Andy Rain/epa).
Getty Images: 10 (Keystone/Hulton Archive), 12 (Roger Viollet).
Shutterstock: 8 (Sam DCruz).

Cover pictures:
Foreground: A Japanese infant sits crying in the rubble left by the
explosion of the atomic bomb at Hiroshima.
Background: The mushroom cloud over Hiroshima.

Every attempt has been made to clear copyright. Should there be any
inadvertent omission, please apply to the publisher for rectification.

SL001440US   Supplier 02 Date 0512 Print Run 2025

*Having found the bomb we have used it.
We have used it against those who
attacked us without warning ... against
those who have starved and beaten and
executed American prisoners of war ...
We have used it in order to shorten the
agony of war, in order to save the lives of
thousands and thousands of young
Americans.*

President Truman explains his decision to drop the
bomb, August 8, 1945

CONTENTS

1

olonel Paul W. Tibbets Jr. was reckoned the best flier in America. He had even served as personal pilot to General Eisenhower, the future president. So it was no surprise that he was chosen to command the most secret mission the United States had ever undertaken.

Shortly after midnight on August 6, 1945, Tibbets and 11 hand-picked crew members clambered aboard the *Enola Gay*, a modified B-29 Super Fortress based on the Pacific island of Tinian. Tibbets had picked the plane personally, naming it after his mother back in Miami, Florida. Attached to the 509th Composite Group, it featured reduced armor and only one gunner, Sergeant Bob Caron. Bob sat out alone in the tail behind his twin .50 caliber machine guns. Although he didn't know it at the time, he would

play a key role in the operation. His camera would be the only one to take live pictures of the action.

At around 2:45 a.m. the four Wright R3350 engines roared into life and hauled the heavily laden *Enola Gay* along the runway and into the air. Tibbets immediately headed northwest, toward southern Japan. Officially he alone knew the precise purpose of their mission. Behind him, however, Second Lieutenant Morris Jeppson also had a fair idea.

A physicist who had read a secondhand copy of a banned book on nuclear explosions, Jeppson realized that "Little Boy," the 10-ton weapon hanging in the bay beneath them, was not just a "super powerful bomb," as they had been told. The *Enola Gay* was carrying the world's first atomic bomb. Its target was the city of Hiroshima.

All clear for takeoff: the *Enola Gay*, a specially modified B-29 Super Fortress, stands poised on the runway at Tinian before setting out on the most momentous bombing mission in history.

2 THE CITY OF HIROSHIMA

To most people, the word *Hiroshima* means only one thing: the terrifying dawn of the nuclear age. The center of the city was totally destroyed by the bomb that the *Enola Gay* dropped. World War II ended shortly afterward when the Japanese accepted that they faced a weapon against which they had no defense. Untold thousands died in the blast and firestorm that followed, and for years thousands more continued to perish from the effects of radiation. The dark shadow of Hiroshima has hung over the world ever since, a shadow so terrifying that for almost 70 years no nation has dared use nuclear weapons in anger.

Hiroshima Castle, originally built in the 1590s, was obliterated by the nuclear attack of August 6, 1945. The reconstruction shown here was finished 13 years later.

FACT FILE

Mori and Asano

The powerful nobleman Mori Terumoto, head of the Mori clan, founded the city of Hiroshima in 1598. He made it his clan headquarters and cemented his power with a new and impressive castle. Later, in the hands of the Asano clan, Hiroshima expanded and prospered. Asano rule ended in the mid-19th century, when the transformation into the modern industrial port began.

The islands of Japan

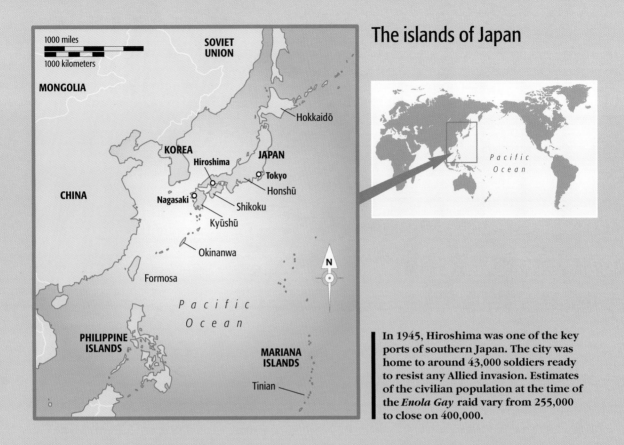

In 1945, Hiroshima was one of the key ports of southern Japan. The city was home to around 43,000 soldiers ready to resist any Allied invasion. Estimates of the civilian population at the time of the *Enola Gay* raid vary from 255,000 to close on 400,000.

From castle to city

Japan is made up of more than 6,800 islands. Just four of them—Honshū, Hokkaidō, Kyūshū, and Shikoku—comprise some 97 percent of the country's land area. The principal island is Honshū, or "Main State." The seventh largest island in the world, it is bigger than Great Britain and only slightly smaller than Kansas. Along Honshū's crowded southeastern coastline are most of Japan's great cities: Tokyo, Kyoto, Osaka, and, at the southern end, Hiroshima.

Hiroshima, meaning "wide island," was founded at the end of the 16th century by Mori Terumoto, a nobleman who built a castle there. Rapid expansion came in the 19th century, when Japan developed into an industrial nation. The sheltered coastal location was ideal for trade and, as railroads, factories, warehouses, and workshops sprang up around the excellent harbor, the city grew fast. Between 1889 and 1929, its population rose from 83,000 to 270,000, making it Japan's seventh most populous city.

Military base

Hiroshima continued to flourish and its transportation system improved with the introduction of electric streetcars. As a result its business and shopping hub moved away from the old castle area toward the docks. Central planning brought new organization to the metropolitan area and the 1930s and early 1940s witnessed a renovation of the port and the use of land reclaimed from the sea.

The busy main street of Hiroshima's Kawaya-cho (now Hondori) district in about 1930. It was at the heart of the city's commercial area.

At the same time, a more ominous development was taking place. From 1931 onward Hiroshima was an important military base. Barracks were constructed to house troops waiting to go abroad, first to serve in China, and then, during the 1940s, in the Japanese Empire. Supplies were kept there, too, and a communications center was established. It was these military installations that made the city a priority target for the *Enola Gay's* devastating attack.

During World War II, many Japanese observers wondered why, when Tokyo and other large cities were attacked so frequently, Hiroshima was left almost unscathed. The reason was horrifyingly simple. Before August 6, 1945, an atomic bomb had been tested only over a desert. No one knew for certain what the effects of exploding one over a city would be. The Hiroshima bombing, therefore, would be an experiment to answer the scientists' questions. Because they wanted their data as clear as possible, they needed a target free from damage by conventional bombing.

So, like mice in a laboratory, Hiroshima and its people were left relatively unharmed so that the true effects of "the big one" could be measured.

Dreadful data

The bomb's detonation provided the scientists and the military with the data they sought. The watching world picked it up, too. After the explosion, Hiroshima was, to all intents and purposes, no more. An entire city had been destroyed. A few days later, another city, Nagasaki, went the same way. Had Japan not surrendered, the unspeakable process might have continued until all the great cities of Japan had been reduced to rubble. The irony is that, had this happened, the United States would still not have been able to invade Japan because the radiation levels there would have been fatal to its own troops as well as the Japanese.

The lessons of what had taken place at Hiroshima were soon learned. Human beings, the intelligent apes that had in a few thousand years mastered the planet, now had the means to wipe themselves out in a few minutes. International relations would never be the same. Warfare would never be the same. The genie that had been released from the bottle could never be put back: A brilliant flash, a thunderous shock wave, and a giant mushroom of dust over Hiroshima had changed the world for ever.

A conventional strike: the port city of Kushiro Hokka is engulfed in smoke and flames after a raid from carrier-based planes of the US Third Fleet on July 14, 1945.

VOICES

A highly secret matter

Dear Mr. President,
I think it is very important that I should have a talk with you as soon as possible on a highly secret matter. I mentioned it to you shortly after you took office but have not urged it since on account of the pressure you have been under. It, however, has such a bearing on our present foreign relations and has such an important effect upon all my thinking in this field that I think you ought to know about it without much further delay.

Faithfully yours,
Henry Stimson
Secretary of War

A letter from Secretary of War Henry Stimson to President Harry Truman about the existence of the A-bomb, April 24, 1945

3. THE PACIFIC WAR

The bombings of Hiroshima and Nagasaki in the summer of 1945 were the final acts in a war that had started in China eight years earlier. Some argue that the origins of the conflict can be traced back even further, at least to the Japanese seizure of Manchuria in the early 1930s.

Nevertheless, the direct path to Hiroshima lay through the war that broke out between the United States and Japan in December 1941. At this time, though, mesmerized by the surprise attack that had begun the conflict, no one on either side could have dreamed of the even more astonishing way it would be brought to a close.

VOICES

Remarkable progress

By comparing the Japan of 50 years ago with the Japan of today, it will be seen that she has gained considerably in the extent of her territory, as well as in her population ... In commerce and industry ... she has also made rapid strides ... Her general progress ... has been so sudden and swift that it presents a rare spectacle in the history of the world.

Okuma, *Fifty Years of New Japan*, 1910

Japanese modernization and expansion

Until the mid-19th century, Japan deliberately cut itself off from the rest of the world. Then, seeing its poor industrial and commercial position compared with Western nations, it began to modernize rapidly.

The first Mazda vehicles roll off the production line in Hiroshima, 1937.

FACT FILE

Timeline: the expansion of the Japanese Empire

1895	• Taiwan
1905	• Korea (an official colony in 1910) • Southern Sakhalin • Port Arthur • South Manchurian Railroad
1919	• Shandong
1931–2	• Manchuria
1937 onward	• North-east and eastern China
1940 onward	• Indochina
1941 onward	• Southeast Asia and Pacific islands

By the early 1900s Japan was powerful enough to seize Taiwan (Formosa) from China, occupy Korea, and take territory from Russia. Even by this early date, the United States was keeping a close eye on Japanese ambitions. It was particularly keen to retain an "open door" for all nations to trade with China.

Having previously gained control over the South Manchurian Railroad, in 1931 the Japanese military used the excuse of a sabotage attack at Mukden to occupy the entire northern Chinese province of Manchuria. The United States and the League of Nations objected but did not intervene. Six years later, again exploiting a minor incident, Japanese forces in China launched an all-out war and soon occupied huge swathes of the north and east of the country. By now the United States was deeply concerned.

Victims of empire-building: citizens of Chungking, China, made homeless by the Japanese attack of May 1939, walk past the burning ruins of their city.

Japan and the United States at war

Japan's government faced two serious problems. First, it was unable to control the military. Especially on the Asian mainland, army officers launched policies of their own with scant regard to Tokyo. Second, key positions in many walks of life were held by men who rejected democratic values and instead embraced more traditional virtues of military glory and unquestioning loyalty to the emperor. Worryingly, Japan was coming increasingly under the influence of the military.

Seeking fuel and minerals, in September 1940 Japan began to create an Asian empire by invading French Indochina (Vietnam, Cambodia, and Laos). President Franklin Roosevelt responded with economic sanctions. The following summer, as the Japanese continued their Asian empire-building, US sanctions tightened to include fuel oil. Believing war with the United States was now inevitable, Japan's commanders planned a devastating first strike.

FACT FILE

US economic power

World War II ended the Great Depression in the United States, which had dominated the 1930s; the war also doubled the country's manufacturing output. GDP (Gross Domestic Product—the total value of goods and services) rose from $91 billion to $166.6 billion between 1939 and 1945, as factories delivered the thousands of tanks, aircraft, and guns demanded by the military. To pay for it all, by 1944 almost all workers were paying federal income tax, compared with just 10 percent in 1939.

On December 7, 1941, a Japanese task force launched a surprise attack on Pearl Harbor, the US Navy's Hawaiian base. All but one of the battleships there were sunk or put out of action. The United States declared war on Japan the following day.

After Pearl Harbor, the Japanese extended their empire across the Philippines, Malaya, Indonesia, and into Burma. Farther east, they overwhelmed several Pacific islands and pushed on toward New Guinea, threatening Australia. Japanese expansion was finally slowed on May 4–8, 1942. America's carriers had survived Pearl Harbor and in the Coral Sea they spearheaded a counterattack. Although the United States suffered heavier casualties than the enemy, the Japanese were forced to postpone their invasion of New Guinea. Within a year that postponement had become a cancellation.

The United States on the offensive

America's first decisive victory over Japan came at the Battle of Midway on June 3–6, 1942. Admiral Yamamoto, supreme commander of the Japanese fleet, hoped to seize Midway, the most remote island in the Hawaiian atoll, and from there take control of the eastern Pacific. US intelligence obtained advance warning of the plan and set up an ambush.

The battle, conducted entirely by aircraft, was the first fought by two fleets out of sight of each other. The United States enjoyed some good fortune when its bombers, following a Japanese destroyer, caught the Japanese carriers with their planes being refueled on deck between missions. Three carriers were sunk and a fourth went down later. By the time the fight ended, the Japanese had lost several more ships, nearly 270 aircraft, and some 3,500 men. US losses were much lower and the country was now in a position to begin its offensive across the Pacific toward Japan.

Infamous day

Yesterday, December 7, 1941—a date which will live in infamy - the United States of America was suddenly and deliberately attacked by naval and air forces of the Empire of Japan … I assert that … this form of treachery shall never endanger us again … With confidence in our armed forces— with the unbounded determination of our people—we will gain the inevitable triumph.

President Franklin Delano Roosevelt, December 8, 1941

It's war! The wrecks of the battleships USS *West Virginia* and *Tennessee* burn fiercely after a surprise Japanese attack had caught the US fleet in Pearl Harbor completely off guard.

The strategy adopted by Admiral Chester Nimitz, the US commander-in-chief, was known as "island hopping." He believed it would prove the quickest way to bring Japanese cities within range of his heavy bombers. The war would ultimately be won, he reckoned, by destroying the enemy's capacity to produce armaments. To some extent this strategy was correct. In the end, though, it was more than the destruction of factories, docks, and other installations that forced the Japanese to surrender.

The struggle across the Pacific was long, gruelling, and extremely bloody. The recapture of the Solomon Islands (1942–3) cost the lives of 10,600 Americans and 80,000 Japanese. Another 1,800 Americans died retaking the Gilbert and Marshall Islands (1943–4), 9,500 in the Marianas campaign, 6,821 on Iwo Jima (1945), and another 12,500 on Okinawa. Total Japanese losses came close to 300,000 killed, with perhaps a similar number of deaths among noncombatants and civilians. Alarmingly, by 1945 increasing numbers of Japanese soldiers were choosing to die rather than accept the indignity of surrender.

The bombing of Japan

In the early summer of 1944, B-29s flying from China started pounding Japan's cities with high explosives. After the Marianas were taken in July, the bombers operated from there. Precision bombing was difficult from high altitude and enemy production suffered less from US action than from the relocation of factories into the countryside. Consequently, in January 1945, US tactics changed. The B-29s came in low, one at a time, and dropped mostly incendiary bombs. The targets were now not individual factories or docks but entire cities and their civilian populations.

Fire-bomb attacks on buildings of largely wooden construction, sometimes also incorporating paper, had a devastating effect. The attack on Tokyo on the night of February 24–25, 1945, for example, laid waste

Action on Okinawa, 1945: US soldiers flush out a Japanese sniper as they consolidate their position on the island before preparing to move on to Honshū.

The Big Three, Yalta 1945: (left to right) Churchill, Roosevelt, and Stalin at the meeting during which Stalin promised Soviet help in the war against Japan.

740 acres (300 hectares) of the city. Worse was to come. On the night of March 9–10, 285 B-29s unloaded 2,000 metric tons of incendiaries on the Japanese capital. Fanned by the high wind, the firestorm killed more than 80,000 people and obliterated the downtown area. Such was the ferocious appetite of the blaze that it sucked people and even whole buildings into its flaming maw.

Despite the terrible losses and the unimaginable suffering, the Japanese government refused to contemplate surrender. What was the US president to do? A full-scale invasion of Japan, he was told, would cost an estimated one million US casualties. By mid-1945, however, he had another option.

FACT FILE

The Yalta Conference

In February 1945, at Yalta on the Black Sea, the Allied leaders—Josef Stalin (Soviet Union), Franklin Roosevelt (United States), and Winston Churchill (Great Britain)—discussed the postwar world. Roosevelt welcomed Stalin's decision to enter the war against Japan after Germany's defeat. Later, unwilling for Japanese territory to fall into Soviet hands, the United States regretted this decision. Using the atomic bomb was a way of ending the war quickly, before their communist allies advanced too far.

4 DECISION TIME

World War II broke out in Europe in 1939, less than a year after scientists had proved that nuclear fission—splitting an atom—was practicable and that the process might release tremendous energy. Controlled, this energy could serve to generate heat and electricity. In an uncontrolled "chain reaction," it could produce a terrific explosion. Because of the war, developing the explosive potential of this new technology took priority, and so began the race to produce the world's first nuclear bomb.

The theory

In the early 20th century the great physicist Albert Einstein (1879–1955) showed that mass (matter or physical substance) could be transformed into energy. In order to release the energy, scientists had to split apart the building blocks of matter, called atoms. At the center of every atom is a cluster of particles known as the nucleus. Splitting the nucleus of an atom proved to be the key to releasing some of its mass as energy.

To build a bomb, the scientists aimed to create a fission chain reaction (*fission* means "splitting"). This meant that when an atom was split, the particles given off would split the nuclei of other atoms, which would split still others, and so on. The chain reaction could only be achieved by using certain rare forms (or isotopes) of radioactive materials such as uranium and plutonium. Radioactive materials are materials that emit energy in the form of streams of particles. They do this because of the decay of their unstable atoms.

The Manhattan Project

In August 1939 President Roosevelt, acting on the advice of Albert Einstein, set up a Uranium Committee to oversee America's nuclear investigations. By 1942 this committee had expanded into the Manhattan Project. The project's top-secret aim was to produce a nuclear weapon in the shortest possible time.

The Manhattan Project operated from sites in Washington, Tennessee, and New Mexico. In Oak Ridge, Tennessee, an entire new township was built, swelling from around 3,000 inhabitants in 1942 to nearly 75,000 by 1945. Despite Oak Ridge's rapid growth, its security fences and guard towers, and the construction there of the world's largest building, the site's purpose remained a mystery to outsiders. Even many of its employees did not know what they were engaged in. By mid-1944, the Manhattan Project was costing $100 million a month—and there was still no certainty that it would produce a bomb.

(right) **The genius behind the bomb: Albert Einstein, the brilliant physicist, who showed that it was possible for a small amount of matter to be converted into a vast amount of energy.**

VOICES

Albert Einstein alerts President Roosevelt

Sir: I believe … it is my duty to bring to your attention the following … It may be possible to set up a nuclear chain reaction in a large mass of uranium, by which vast amounts of power … would be generated … This [might] also lead to the construction of extremely powerful bombs … A single bomb of this type … exploded in a port might very well destroy the whole port together with some of the surrounding territory.

August 2, 1939

The test

Doubts dissolved over the winter of 1944–5. By the spring the team was close to making two bombs: one using an isotope of uranium called uranium-235 and another, even more powerful, using an isotope of plutonium. Following the sudden death of Franklin Roosevelt in April 1945, Harry Truman became president and was briefed on the Manhattan Project. Key decisions had to be made. Should other nations be told about the bomb? Which Japanese sites would make the most suitable targets? Truman decided to keep the bomb a secret while advisors examined possible targets. Hiroshima topped their list.

On May 7, a small test explosion was carried out. Then came the main test of a full nuclear bomb at the Alamogordo Test Range south of Los Alamos, New Mexico, on July 16, 1945. At 5:30 a.m. a plutonium bomb was detonated on top of a steel tower. Scientists estimated that the explosion would be equivalent to around 5,000 tons of TNT. They were hopelessly wrong: The blast was nearer 18,600 tons. The tower vaporized instantaneously within a massive crater of radioactive glass. Observers peering through colored lenses were temporarily blinded by the flash, and the blast shattered windows 120 miles (200 kilometers) away. Then, swelling like an Old Testament plague, a gigantic mushroom cloud rose 7 miles (12 kilometers) over the dusty desert. The atomic age was born.

A blurred photograph of the first ever nuclear explosion, July 16, 1945. The force of the blast in the desert of New Mexico shocked the experts, including the photographer.

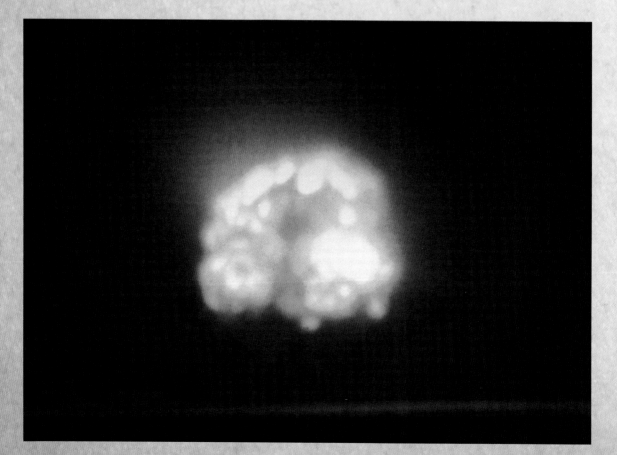

Wrong decision

It is my opinion that the use of this barbarous weapon at Hiroshima and Nagasaki was of no material assistance in our war against Japan. The Japanese were already defeated and ready to surrender because of the effective sea blockade and the successful bombing with conventional weapons.

Admiral William D. Leahy, 1950

Lost in wonder, shock, and horror, scientists and military personnel examine the vaporized remains of the steel tower that had held the first nuclear bomb.

No surrender

President Truman could have decided to test the bomb openly on a deserted island, demonstrating to all the world its terrible destructive power. A major reason why he chose not to do this was the fiercely proud culture of the enemy, for whom surrender would be an almost unbearable disgrace. Many Japanese believed, like the kamikaze pilots who flew their bomb-laden planes straight into US warships, that death was better than capture. This attitude helps explain Japan's ill-treatment of Allied prisoners of war. The Japanese had no respect for those who had given up the fight. US soldiers advancing across the Pacific met the same resolute mentality when thousands of Japanese, faced with inevitable defeat, chose to perish rather than lay down their arms.

The position of the Japanese emperor, Hirohito, was also crucial. In fact the term *emperor* does not really do justice to the role. In Japanese, the title of emperor means "heavenly king," illustrating how his role was both religious and political. He was the heart and soul of his country and all Japanese citizens owed him absolute obedience. A Japan without an emperor was unthinkable. So, when Allied diplomats failed to guarantee the emperor's safety if Japan surrendered, his people had little choice but to fight on.

21

Truman's decision

President Truman was at Potsdam, near the shattered German capital of Berlin, when he learned of the successful nuclear bomb test. He was meeting with the British and the Soviets to discuss the future of Europe and how to defeat Japan. The news from New Mexico changed everything. No longer needing Soviet help in the Far East, the United States now wanted to finish the war before Stalin joined it. Soviet secret agents may actually have already informed their leader of what was happening: When Truman told Stalin that he had a "powerful new weapon," his ally showed little surprise.

Truman did not have to use the atomic bomb. He could have continued with the conventional bombing of Japan (which the US Air Force predicted would flatten all major cities by January 1, 1946) and gone ahead with the invasion planned for November 1. But Truman was concerned by the estimated one million US casualties that such an undertaking might incur. He decided instead to drop the atomic bomb on a Japanese city. This, the president hoped, would shock the Japanese into surrendering.

Preparation for the attack

On July 25 Tibbets's 509th Composite Group was placed at the ready and USS *Indianapolis* shipped the components of a uranium bomb—untested—to the Pacific island of Tinian. The following day the Allied powers issued the Potsdam Declaration, warning Japan to accept unconditional surrender or face the "utter devastation of the Japanese homeland." Some members of the Japanese government were prepared to consider such terms; however, as the ultimatum did not guarantee the emperor's safety, the decision went against them.

FACT FILE

"Kill with silence"

Japan's response to the Potsdam Declaration of July 26, 1945, has fascinated historians. Prime Minister Suzuki, speaking to the Japanese press, used the word *mokusatsu*. This was translated as "kill with silence," although it can also mean "pass over in silence" or "ignore." Despite the fact that Suzuki spoke of fighting on, there is evidence that Japan might have been persuaded to surrender without the need for the United States to carry out an A-bomb attack.

For the first few days of August bad weather kept the *Enola Gay* on the ground. Then, on the 5th, the skies cleared. That night Tibbets and his crew took off in the plane and set its automatic pilot on a course toward their target. They would arrive, the navigator estimated, shortly after dawn. Just as the citizens of Hiroshima were getting ready for a new day.

Planning the top-secret mission: US flight crews at the Tinian base go over the plans one last time.

Unfazed by his momentous mission, Colonel Paul W. Tibbets waves from the cockpit of the *Enola Gay* shortly before takeoff on August 6, 1945.

5 THE ATTACK

The bomb that changed the world: a replica of "Little Boy," the first nuclear weapon used in anger, at the United States Air Force Museum and National Aviation Hall of Fame in Dayton, Ohio.

FACT FILE

"Little Boy"

The precise details of the atomic bomb dropped on Hiroshima are still secret in case they help the unauthorized manufacture of a nuclear weapon. The device was 10.9 feet (3.3 meters) long, 2 feet (60 centimeters) in diameter, and weighed around 5 tons (4.6 metric tons). The gigantic explosion it caused came from the transformation into energy of just 1.3 pounds (0.6 kilograms) of the 140 pounds (64 kilograms) of uranium-235 it contained.

The *Enola Gay's* long flight to Japan passed without a hitch. Meeting up with two other B-29s—*Great Artiste*, carrying blast measuring equipment, and the camera-laden Plane No. 91 (later named *Necessary Evil*)—it flew at low level over Iwo Jima, then turned northwest toward southern Honshū. In case it exploded prematurely, if the *Enola Gay* crashed on takeoff, "Little Boy" was not armed for detonation until well into the flight. About 45 minutes before reaching the Japanese coastline, the crew was told that the cloud cover over Hiroshima was thin: the target was confirmed.

Eight fifteen

To lessen the danger of interception by enemy fighters and antiaircraft fire, Tibbets took his plane up to 30,800 feet (9,400 meters). This also prevented the *Enola Gay* from being destroyed by the explosion of its own bomb. Shortly afterward, the crew checked visually that they were over Hiroshima and Tibbets steered for the T-shaped Aioi Bridge at the center of the target area.

At 8:15 a.m. local time Bombardier Tom Ferebee released the bomb. Suddenly lightened, the *Enola Gay* lurched upwards. Within seconds Tibbets had put his plane into a screaming dive and wrenched it into a 155-degree turn. He had 43 seconds to get as far away as possible.

Flash, fire, and blast

To maximize its effect, "Little Boy" was detonated automatically 1,900 feet (580 meters) above the ground. First came the flash, a light brighter than many suns that burned out the eyes of those looking toward it. Almost instantaneously a 7,160°F (3,980°C) fireball engulfed ground zero (the area directly beneath the explosion) and the surrounding area. Houses, trees, bicycles, people, pets—everything in its path—was vaporized or incinerated in an instant. A tremendous shockwave, traveling faster than the speed of sound, roared after the fire. It was, said survivors, like a thunderstorm created by the Devil to destroy the earth. Within a two-mile (3.2-kilometre) wide circle of annihilation, hardly a building was left standing. All structures suffered damage up to three miles (4.8 kilometers) away. The weaker ones, especially those of wooden construction, were flattened.

Frozen in time: this pocket watch, found on the body of a victim of the A-bomb dropped on Hiroshima, will always read 8:15 a.m., the moment the bomb exploded.

VOICES

What have we done?

A pinprick of purplish light expands to a glowing fireball hundreds of feet wide ... On board nobody speaks ... Looking down was like a peep into Hell ... The mushroom is maybe a mile or two wide and a mile high. It's very black, but there is a purplish tint to the cloud. The base is shot through with flames. The city must be below that. My God what have we done?

Written record of co-pilot Robert Lewis

Spreading rapidly out from the center with an intensity even more ghastly than that caused by conventional bombing, the firestorm eventually devoured 4.4 square miles (11.4 square kilometers) of the city. It was noted that very few survivors had leg injuries. The reason was simple: Thousands who had been crippled by the blast were cremated alive. Within 30 minutes around half Hiroshima's population, including 90 percent of its doctors, had been killed or injured.

Relief, radiation, and reward

It was several hours before the Japanese government fully realized what had happened. All they knew was that at 8:16 a.m. Hiroshima's phones had gone dead, the radio station had stopped broadcasting, and all transportation to and from the city had suddenly ceased. Then, gradually,

reports began to come in of a terrible explosion. A scout plane sent to review the damage reported a huge pillar of smoke and dust hanging over the city. It was visible from more than 100 miles (160 kilometers) away.

Slowly, struggling with the chaos and unprecedented scale of the disaster, relief parties began to work their way through the wreckage. As the bodies that had not been incinerated were buried and the sick and injured given such medical help as was available, a fresh horror dawned: radiation.

VOICES

What had happened?

The hour was early; the morning still, warm, and beautiful. Shimmering leaves reflected sunlight from a cloudless sky … Suddenly, a strong flash of light startled me—and then another … Garden shadows disappeared. The view … was now dark and hazy … I tried to escape, but … a profound weakness overcame me … What had happened? All over the right side of my body I was cut and bleeding.

Hiroshima survivor Dr. Michihiko Hachiya

Symbol of doom: a gigantic mushroom cloud rises over Hiroshima immediately after the obliteration of the city in the early morning of August 6, 1945.

A once thriving and busy city is reduced to rubble and ashes: an aerial view of Hiroshima a few days after the nuclear attack.

Radioactive contamination distorts the blood and destroys the bone marrow's ability to produce a healthy replacement. It also severely damages the body's internal organs, especially the liver. In the longer term it induces many types of cancer. Untold thousands died as a result of radiation, some only hours after exposure, some days later, and some after many years. Since radiation levels within a mile (1.6 kilometers) of ground zero remained dangerously high for several weeks, radiation sickness killed many from the rescue services.

Meanwhile, back at Tinian, the returning crew of the *Enola Gay* were welcomed as heroes. As Tibbets stepped proudly from his plane, a delighted senior officer pinned a gleaming medal to his chest: the Distinguished Service Cross.

FACT FILE

Unknown toll

No one knows how many people "Little Boy" killed. It seems likely that between 40,000 and 60,000 died within a few seconds of it exploding, and perhaps twice that number were injured. Thousands of others died in the firestorm and of their injuries and from radiation sickness. Estimates of the total number of deaths range from 90,000 to 202,000. The US Department of Energy put the figure at around 200,000.

6. NAGASAKI AND SURRENDER

While shattered local authorities were trying to come to terms with what had happened at Hiroshima and to organize rescue and relief programs, President Truman was telling the world of the first-ever nuclear attack. He also threatened that if Japan did not accept the terms of the Potsdam Declaration (the Allied ultimatum of July 26, 1945) and offer an unconditional surrender, more atomic bombs would be dropped. The United States would, he promised, "obliterate" every factory, dock, and workshop throughout the land. The president gave the impression that he had a large number of bombs at his immediate disposal, which was not true. There were just two more bombs, the second of which would not be ready for at least a month. Surprisingly, with radiation deaths in Hiroshima soaring, it was two days before Japan's ministers met to discuss what to do next.

Disagreement and the Soviets

At the highest level, Japanese reaction to the Hiroshima bombing was mixed. Prime Minister Suzuki and Foreign Minister Togo

The plutonium weapon dropped on Nagasaki, nicknamed "Fat Man," was even more powerful than the uranium bomb dropped on Hiroshima.

FACT FILE

"Fat Man"

The second atomic bomb—a plutonium bomb dropped on the city of Nagasaki—was called "Fat Man," which was possibly a reference to Winston Churchill. As its name suggests, "Fat Man" looked very different from "Little Boy." Roughly the same length and weight, it was twice as wide, with a diameter of 5 feet (1.5 meters). This was because it detonated when 32 explosive charges forced a sphere of plutonium in on itself. Under great pressure, the element's density increased sufficiently to begin a nuclear reaction.

Shigenori believed it was time to surrender in order to prevent further loss of life. Admiral Soemu Toyoda, the chief of the Naval General Staff, said the United States could not have made more than two or three bombs, so Japan should fight on. Army commanders shared this view. Behind the scenes, Emperor Hirohito and his closest advisor, Marquis Koichi Kido, appeared to agree with the prime minister.

Early in the morning of August 9 Japan's military position suddenly grew worse. The Soviet Union, previously neutral in the war in the Far East, declared war on Japan and invaded Manchuria. Even if Japan had been able to repel a US invasion, as some generals had argued it could, resisting a two-pronged attack was inconceivable. Victory of any kind was now absolutely

Japanese-trained troops in Manchuria (which the Japanese renamed "Manchukuo" after they had taken it over) prepare to resist a Russian invasion.

impossible. This left the Japanese leadership with a stark choice: surrender or face total annihilation. Given the long tradition of honorable death in Japanese culture, a number of army officers were still rejecting the humiliation of surrender.

Nagasaki

Having received the news from Manchuria, the Japanese cabinet realized that the game was up. The only major disagreement was whether to accept Potsdam at once or to seek a guarantee that the emperor would not be harmed or insulted. The United States was not aware of these discussions. Nevertheless, it neither waited for the Japanese to react to the Soviet attack nor asked whether, now they had witnessed Hiroshima, they would accept the ultimatum. Instead, it launched a second nuclear strike. The target this time would be the city of Nagasaki.

President Truman did not specifically authorize the use of the Nagasaki bomb, although he could have stopped it. In late July the president had given a general go-ahead to military commanders to use nuclear weapons as soon as they were ready. On August 9 a B-29 named *Bock's Car*, commanded by Major Charles W. Sweeney, left Tinian at 3:47 a.m. Nagasaki was not the intended target. Sweeney's instructions were to bomb Kokura Arsenal, a huge complex of factories and other industrial plant near the city of Kokura.

Unlike the *Enola Gay* bomb run, however, the *Bock's Car* mission was plagued with problems. Rough weather battered the plane on the way to Japan; one of the two observation B-29s arrived an hour late while the second never showed up at all; and a pall of smoke and cloud hung over Kokura. With enemy fighters and antiaircraft fire making the situation more perilous by the minute, Major Sweeney switched the attack to the secondary target of Nagasaki. Here, using radar and peering through the cloud cover to get a fix on the target, *Bock's Car* dropped its plutonium bomb, "Fat Man," at 11:02 a.m. The bomb exploded less than a minute later about 1,650 feet (500 meters) above the ground.

FACT FILE

Nagasaki

Nagasaki is a large port on the island of Kyūshū. It was founded in the 16th century by Portuguese missionaries and grew into a cosmopolitan trading city. During the 20th century Nagasaki became a center of heavy industry and shipbuilding. Many Japanese naval vessels were built there, making it a major target for Allied bombing in World War II.

Trying to rebuild his life, a Japanese civilian pushes his bike down a path cleared through the rubble of Hiroshima. The threat from radiation, not clearly understood at the time, remained serious for weeks after the explosion.

Surrender

Although "Fat Man" exploded with considerably more force than "Little Boy," it caused less damage because Nagasaki's hills sheltered some districts from the blast. Even so, the destruction and loss of life were horrific. All but 12 percent of the city's homes were destroyed or damaged. Around 40,000 people died instantly and 60,000 were injured. As at Hiroshima, radiation sickness ensured that the death toll rose for a long time afterward. Within six months it had topped 70,000, and stood at nearly 150,000 after five years.

The Japanese cabinet received news of the Nagasaki bombing in the middle of a meeting. Discussions continued long into the night, finally involving the emperor himself. In the end, it seems, it was his decision to "bear the unbearable" that finally persuaded the Japanese government to accept the Allies' ultimatum. However, even now Japan's reply stated that it could not accept anything undermining the position of the emperor.

> # VOICES
>
> ## *To die is easy but to live is difficult*
>
> *[The position] is beyond our reasoning …I believe that the national politics and the supreme military command should be in harmony. There is no hope left for us for the continuation of the war, now with the dropping of the atomic bombs and the Soviet Union joining the war …To die is easy but to live is difficult.*
>
> Minister Sakuri at a cabinet meeting, August 14, 1945

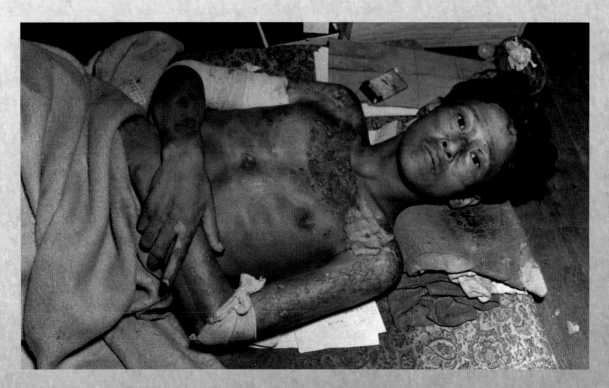

| The body of a young victim of the Nagasaki nuclear bomb is covered with dreadful burns. The radiation to which he had been exposed was probably even more dangerous.

The Allies' response to this gave nothing away, stating simply that Japan's new form of government would be chosen by its people. The Japanese cabinet hesitated. To help it make up its mind, on August 14 Truman ordered hostilities to be resumed: Warships bombarded Japan's coast and 1,014 aircraft rained further death and destruction on its cities. Once again the Japanese cabinet met. This time, with the emperor's blessing, it agreed to accept the Potsdam Declaration unconditionally. Hirohito recorded a disc of a speech to be played to his people ordering them to surrender.

VOICES

Surrender at last

To our good and loyal subjects: After pondering deeply the general trends of the world and the actual conditions obtaining in our empire today, we have decided to effect a settlement of the present situation by resorting to an extraordinary measure. We have ordered our Government to communicate to the Governments of the United States, Great Britain, China, and the Soviet Union that our empire accepts the provisions of their joint declaration.

Emperor Hirohito accepts the Allies' Potsdam Declaration, August 15, 1945

On the deck of the USS *Missouri*, General Umezu signs Japan's surrender on behalf of his country's military administration. The civilian government also signed.

The failed coup

When they heard about this, a small group of army officers attempted a coup in order to prevent the announcement being made. Late on August 14 a number of junior Japanese army officers, led by Major Kenji Hatanaka, broke into the Imperial Palace, hoping to find and destroy the recording of Hirohito's surrender speech. No senior figures joined them, however, and by the early morning of August 15 the coup had fizzled out. Its leaders committed suicide. The emperor's speech was broadcast across Japan at noon.

Terms and trials

VJ (Victory in Japan) Day saw widespread rejoicing throughout the Allied nations, especially in the United States, New Zealand, and Australia. The mood in Japan was understandably different. A few days later Douglas MacArthur, the supreme commander of the Allied Powers in the Far East, met with Japanese officials and planned his occupation of the Japanese islands. On September 2 a formal Japanese surrender was signed in Tokyo Bay on board the battleship USS *Missouri*.

In accordance with the terms of the Potsdam Declaration, the Allies put on trial those Japanese they believed responsible for "crimes against peace," "war crimes," and "crimes against humanity." Long prison sentences were handed down and seven men were executed. Asian countries previously occupied by the Japanese also held trials, which resulted in many more death sentences. No charges were leveled against the Japanese royal family, and the emperor kept his title and honored position.

A Japanese soldier demonstrates to a postwar military tribunal how a captured US pilot, Second Lieutenant Darwin T. Emry, had been beheaded. Such treatment was against the rules of war, making all those involved guilty of a war crime.

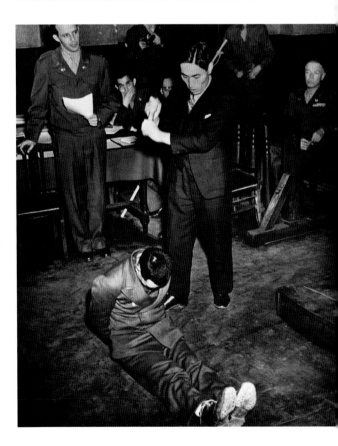

7 THE NUCLEAR AGE

Japan's recovery from the devastation of World War II was little short of miraculous. Within 20 years the country was again a major industrial and commercial power, providing goods, especially automobiles and electrical products, that attracted worldwide respect.

Elsewhere, though, the legacy of Hiroshima was less easily set aside. The A-bomb had ushered in a new phase of warfare, one in which all-out conflict would be devastating for both winners and losers. Sadly, this ghastly fact did not prevent nations from preparing for a third, and final, world war. For more than 40 years (1947–90) the nuclear-armed, capitalist West, headed by the United States, confronted the nuclear-armed, communist East, headed by the Soviet Union. Fortunately for the planet, this terrifying "Cold War" never flared into a full-scale shooting conflict that would have ended human civilization.

Japan reborn

The war cost Japan one quarter of its national wealth. Even rice production, the most basic and essential of services, had fallen by a third. Recovery, however, was remarkably rapid. Not having to waste money on armaments helped—the new constitution of 1947 made Japan a demilitarized state. More important was a general determination to restore national pride through economic rather than military success. The United States, which saw Japan as a key player in its battle against Soviet and Chinese communism, poured money into the country directly and indirectly. The US$550 million grant given to the Philippines, for instance, was earmarked for spending on Japanese imports.

In a peculiar way, wartime destruction and suffering also aided Japan. Its people were accustomed to working long hours for low wages, often in tough conditions. Moreover, its brand-new factories and other industrial plant were of the latest design and often more efficient than those of its competitors. This helped businesses such as Nissan, Toyota, and Sony become household names around the world. Between 1953 and 1970 the rate of Japanese industrial growth averaged a remarkable 10 percent a year. Over the same period the United States managed just over three percent. Today, despite economic difficulties in recent years, Japan boasts the second largest economy in the world.

The task of reconstruction was toughest of all in Hiroshima. First came the immediate work of gathering and burning the bodies of the slain, feeding those who had survived, and restoring basic communications. In the midst of all this, on September 17, a fresh disaster struck. A ferocious typhoon hit what was left of the city, flooding it and claiming a further 3,000 victims. Many of the temporary shelters in which the population had been living were destroyed.

Out of the ashes: nine years after the city had been laid to waste by a nuclear bomb, Hiroshima is being rebuilt, house by house, block by block, district by district.

Showing astounding resilience, Hiroshima's wretched citizens picked themselves up and started all over again. Rubble was cleared, the ground surveyed (a process that took four years) and rebuilding begun. In 1945 experts had predicted that radiation would render the site uninhabitable for another 70 years. They were proved wrong. Special government funding enabled houses, shops, factories, and wharves to rise from the ashes. On the wasteland of ground zero a Peace Memorial Park was laid out.

Cold War

The United States and the Soviet Union had been uneasy allies during World War II. The United States was a democratic-capitalist state run on principles of individual freedom and private enterprise;

VOICES

Never again

We, the Japanese people, acting through our duly elected representatives, … determined that we shall secure for ourselves and our posterity the fruits of peaceful cooperation with all nations and the blessings of liberty throughout this land, and resolved that never again shall we be visited with the horrors of war through the action of government, do proclaim that sovereign power resides with the people and do firmly establish this Constitution.

Preface to Japan's new constitution, November 1946

the communist Soviet Union was founded on the idea that competition between individuals did not benefit the majority and it was the job of an all-controlling government to maintain equality of wealth and opportunity. Both sides—the United States and its allies (the "West") and the Soviet Union and its allies (the "East")—believed the other was seeking world domination. To prevent this from happening, so the argument ran, they needed to be constantly prepared to defend themselves by force. After Hiroshima, that meant maintaining a supply of nuclear weapons.

For four years the West's exclusive possession of A-bombs gave it the upper hand. At times of crisis, as in June 1948 when the Soviets blockaded Berlin, the bomb gave the West the trump card. Then, in September 1949, the position suddenly changed. Much to the surprise of President Truman, the Soviet Union exploded an atomic bomb of its own. This development triggered an "arms race" as each side sought to outdo the other in its stockpile of weaponry.

In 1952 the United States detonated its first H-bomb (hydrogen bomb). This worked in a similar way to the A-bomb except that instead of splitting atoms apart (fission), it fused them together (fusion). The H-bomb had an explosive power a thousand times greater than that of "Little Boy."

FACT FILE

Hiroshima's protest

Postwar Hiroshima was reborn as a "peace memorial city." Ever since, its government has been at the forefront of moves to abolish all nuclear weapons from the planet. Any government anywhere that explodes a nuclear device immediately receives a letter of protest from Hiroshima. Its message is simple: listen to us—we know.

The arms race

In the arms race the two superpowers competed to build ever more powerful nuclear weapons, as well as increasingly sophisticated ways of delivering them. The bombs themselves developed rapidly.

Two young citizens of Hiroshima, survivors of the 1945 atomic bomb, demonstrate for peace on the steps of City Hall, New York City, in 1962.

Soviet missiles parade past the Kremlin, Moscow, home of the Soviet government, during an impressive display of military strength— conventional as well as nuclear.

FACT FILE

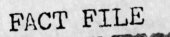

Nuclear arms race

This table illustrates US and Soviet nuclear capacity between 1964 and 1982. The figures show each country's total capacity of nuclear weapons in megatons (millions of tons of TNT). As a comparison, the explosive power released by "Little Boy" was around 15 kilotons (thousands of tons of TNT).

Year	United States	Soviet Union
1964	7,500	1,000
1966	5,600	1,200
1968	5,100	2,300
1970	4,300	3,100
1972	4,100	4,000
1974	3,800	4,200
1976	3,700	4,500
1978	3,800	5,400
1980	4,000	5,700
1982	4,100	7,100

Nine months later the Soviets had an H-bomb of their own. Within a few years there were sufficient bombs stockpiled on either side to wipe out the entire human race, if not from a direct bomb blast then certainly from the appalling levels of radiation that would follow.

Methods of delivering nuclear bombs to their targets began with propeller-driven bombers like the B-29 before advancing to bomber jets and then unmanned guided missiles. At first, missiles were housed in fixed silos. Then, in 1960, the United States produced the first submarine-launched missile, Polaris. This introduced the idea of the "second strike." Previously strategists had worked on the assumption that a devastating first strike by one side could wipe out the other before it had a chance to retaliate. The presence of almost undetectable, nuclear-armed submarines deep beneath the oceans meant that the target nation would always be able to retaliate with a strike of its own. It quickly became clear that any nuclear exchange would mean "mutually assured destruction"— an attack by either side would lead to both being wiped out. The acronym for this situation—MAD—was neatly appropriate.

Fortunately, the United States and the Soviet Union never launched a nuclear war. They came horribly close in 1962 when the United States discovered that the Soviets were establishing missile bases on Cuba, only 90 miles (144 kilometers) from the Florida coast. A standoff between the two sides lasted ten tense days before they managed to reach agreement.

The nuclear mushroom

The Cold War ended in 1990. However, this did not remove the threat of a nuclear holocaust. Today five states officially possess nuclear weapons: the United States, Russia, the United Kingdom, France, and China. India, Pakistan and North Korea have tested nuclear devices, and Israel is also known to possess them. It is widely believed that Iran, too, is trying to develop them. The International Atomic Energy Agency (IAEA) is charged with the difficult task of watching out for illegal nuclear technology.

Despite international treaties limiting the number of nuclear weapons and outlawing their spread, it is alleged that Iraq, Syria, and Burma have tried to develop them. The United States has also sited its own nuclear weapons in Canada, Belgium, Germany, Italy, the Netherlands, and Turkey. Only one state, South Africa, has developed such devices then destroyed them.

The shadow of Hiroshima

In short, weapons capable of destroying the planet are still out there, and slowly they are finding their way into more and more hands. Is it only a matter of time before one is used in anger? The shadow of Hiroshima remains.

VOICES

Eve of destruction

The eastern world it is explodin',
Violence flarin', bullets loadin',
You're old enough to kill but not for votin',
You don't believe in war, but what's that gun you're totin',
And even the Jordan river has bodies floatin',
But you tell me over and over and over again my friend,
Ah, you don't believe we're on the eve of destruction.

"Eve of Destruction," written by P. F. Sloan, was one of the most popular protest songs of the 1960s

---

Seoul, June 25, 2009: burning flags and pictures of politicians and missiles, South Koreans protest North Korea's breaking of international law by conducting a nuclear test. The rest of the world has sided with South Korea to prevent the spread of nuclear weapons.

8 LEST WE FORGET

The atomic bombing of Hiroshima was the single most dramatic act in the history of warfare. It marked a defining moment in modern times and remains deeply controversial. Supporters say it ended the war quickly and probably caused fewer casualties than a prolonged conflict would have done. Critics argue that by August 1945 the war was virtually over and Japan was ready to surrender; the use of the A-bomb, therefore, caused grossly unnecessary suffering, mostly for innocent civilians.

The "hotline" would allow the leaders of the two superpowers to speak to each other directly at moments of crisis. The device was introduced to lessen the risk of accidental nuclear war.

Similar arguments apply to the construction and deployment of nuclear weapons since then. Some say they have prevented a Third World War because no nation is prepared to use them; others say they put our world in mortal danger.

Deterrence

As we have seen, during the Cold War the United States and the Soviet Union each built up vast stocks of nuclear weapons. They also declared that, in the last resort, they were prepared to use them. To support this idea, they developed ever more sophisticated

VOICES

Defending deterrence

We must find peace through strength …I urge you to beware the temptation of pride—the temptation of blithely declaring yourselves above it all and label both sides equally at fault, to ignore the facts of history and the aggressive impulses of an evil empire, to simply call the arms race a giant misunderstanding and thereby remove yourself from the struggle between right and wrong and good and evil.

President Ronald Reagan, 1983

ways of delivering them. Nevertheless, the superpowers insisted that their nuclear weapons were for "deterrence"—to deter enemy attack, not for unprovoked use. In other words, because a nuclear war was too terrible to imagine, nuclear weapons and the theoretical willingness to use them actually preserved peace between East and West. As there was no World War III, it has been argued that the theory worked.

Nevertheless, nuclear deterrence was a horrifyingly dangerous game to play. That is why, after the 1962 Cuban Missile Crisis, a "hotline" was established. This was a direct telephone link between the White House and the Kremlin, allowing US and Soviet leaders to speak directly to each other if ever the world stood on the brink of war. Several international treaties were also signed to limit or reduce weapons stocks and lessen the chance of nuclear disaster. These included the Anti-Ballistic Missile Treaty (1972), two Strategic Arms Limitation Treaties (1972 and 1979), and two post-Cold War Strategic Arms Reductions Treaties (1991 and 1993).

President Barack Obama speaks at a United Nations conference in April 2009. Obama led the discussions on how to reduce the number of nuclear weapons worldwide and prevent their spread.

VOICES

A nuclear-free world?

I will lay out an agenda to seek the goal of a world without nuclear weapons ... The spread of nuclear weapons ... could lead to the extermination of any city on the planet ... [and] we can't reduce the threat of a nuclear weapon going off unless those that possess the most nuclear weapons, the United States and Russia, take serious steps to reduce our stockpiles.

President Barack Obama, April 4, 2009

Unconvinced by official statements that nuclear weapons were for deterrence, protestors around the world called for their total abolition. In Cold War Britain, a small and densely populated island that would have been in the front line in a nuclear war, the Campaign for Nuclear Disarmament was backed by many celebrities and attracted widespread support. Numerous books (such as Nevil Shute's *On the Beach*, 1957) and movies (such as *Threads*, 1984) painted grim and depressing pictures of life after nuclear attack.

Using nuclear energy to generate electricity also received a bad press, especially after an accident at the Chernobyl power station in the Soviet Union (1986) allowed harmful radiation to spread over a vast area. Today, however, in the effort to reduce global warming, countries are looking again at nuclear-powered electricity generation. Japan, which already has a nuclear power station directly opposite Hiroshima on Shikoku Island, is planning to build another 13.

Modern Hiroshima, with its famous streetcars— busy, bustling, yet always conscious of its momentous place in history.

Hiroshima today

Within ten years of its destruction, Hiroshima's population had returned to its prewar total. Tall and elegant new buildings flanked broad, busy streets. The city still had its excellent harbors, making it an ideal choice for major exporting and importing companies. Nissan, Toyota, Hitachi, Bridgestone, Nippon Oil, NEC, and other major firms moved in. A first-class university, research institutes, a science park, stadiums, schools, and sports fields all help to make the city what it is today: a prosperous phoenix risen from a wilderness of ashes. Moreover, as generations grew up who had not experienced the war—for whom August 6, 1945, was a date in history rather than a nightmarish memory—the mood of the city changed. The burden of the past lifted; optimism slowly replaced grim resignation.

Yet Hiroshima can never forget, and that summer morning in 1945 remains branded on the city's collective memory. At ground zero in downtown Hiroshima the authorities have laid out a Peace Memorial Park. At its very heart stands the Atomic Bomb Dome. Built in 1915 to house an exhibition, it was about the only building close to ground zero that was not totally flattened. Controversially, the park's designers did not have it repaired but left it as it stood: Lest We Forget.

FACT FILE

The Peace Memorial Park

Built where downtown Hiroshima had been, the Peace Memorial Park is an open green space dotted with monuments, memorials, museums, and lecture halls. Attracting more than a million visitors annually, it hosts a special ceremony on August 6 every year. In 1996 the United Nations designated the park a World Heritage site. Not all countries agreed with this, especially those that had suffered under Japanese occupation. They wanted more mention of the reasons why the A-bomb had been used.

Sixty years on, bright lanterns of peace float gently down the Motoyasu River toward the grim skeleton of the Atomic Bomb Dome in central Hiroshima.

GLOSSARY

A-bomb Atomic bomb.

allegiance Loyalty to a person or state.

Allies, the Britain, France, the United States, and their allies during World War I and World War II.

atoll A circular coral reef or string of coral islands surrounding a lagoon.

barracks Military accommodations.

blockade An organized action to prevent people or goods from entering or leaving a place.

capitalism A form of government that favors free elections and private ownership of property.

Cold War The period of high tension between the United States and the Soviet Union, lasting from 1946 to 1990.

colony A territory owned by a state beyond its borders.

communist Belief in a system in which capitalism is overthrown and the state controls wealth and property.

coup A change of government by force.

demilitarized Without the presence of military forces.

democratic Describing a government in which the people exercise power through elected representatives.

deterrence A strategy of discouraging enemy attack by maintaining sufficient military force to retaliate.

embargo A ban on trade with a particular country.

firestorm An intense fire that fuels itself by drawing in air and surrounding combustible material.

ground zero The site of the detonation of a nuclear explosion, or the point directly beneath it.

H-bomb Hydrogen bomb.

holocaust Wholesale mass destruction.

incendiary bomb Fire bomb.

kamikaze A suicide mission carried out by a World War II Japanese pilot. He would fly his aircraft, packed with explosives, into an enemy target, often a ship.

Kremlin An ancient fortress in Moscow that houses the Russian government. It is often used to mean the government itself.

League of Nations The international organization for peace and cooperation that operated between 1919 and 1946.

Manchuria A province of northeastern China.

nuclear fission The splitting of the nucleus of an atom, usually accompanied by a powerful release of energy.

open door A policy of making sure that trade with a certain state (especially China) was open to everyone.

phoenix A mythological Greek bird that rose from its own ashes after burning to death.

radiation Invisible rays given out by radioactive substances. Radiation is harmful in large doses.

sabotage Destruction of property by civilians, or by enemy agents during wartime.

sanctions Economic measures intended to punish a state or make it change its policies.

silo An underground missile storage place and launch pad.

sniper Someone who shoots at people from a concealed place.

Soviet Union Officially known as the Union of Soviet Socialist Republics (USSR), a communist-ruled federation of 15 republics, dominated by Russia, that lasted from 1922 to 1991.

stockpile A large supply of something.

ultimatum A demand accompanied by a threat to inflict some penalty if the demand is not met.

wharves Landing places where ships may tie up and load or unload.

FURTHER INFORMATION

BOOKS

Days of Change: The Bombing of Hiroshima and Nagasaki by Valerie Bodden (Creative Education, 2007)

Days that Shook the World: Hiroshima by Jason Hook (Wayland, 2002)

The Enola Gay: The B-29 That Dropped the Atomic Bomb on Hiroshima by Norman Polmar (Brassey's, 2004)

How Did It Happen: Hiroshima by R. G. Grant (Franklin Watts, 2005)

What If We Do Nothing? Nuclear Proliferation by Joseph Harris (Franklin Watts, 2009)

Witness to History: Hiroshima by Nathaniel Harris (Heinemann, 2004)

WEBSITES

www.pcf.city.hiroshima.jp/index_e2.html
The site of the Hiroshima Peace Museum: excellent and accessible information and activities from the heart of Hiroshima.

www.cfo.doe.gov/me70/manhattan/index.htm
The Manhattan Project: informative and respectably objective information from the US Department of Energy.

www.exploratorium.edu/nagasaki/mainn.html
Nagasaki remembered: a moving collection of first-hand memories and photographs.

www.gwu.edu/~nsarchiv/NSAEBB/NSAEBB162/index.htm
Primary sources collected at the US National Security Archive.

www.eyewitnesstohistory.com/hiroshima.htm
Two powerful eyewitness accounts of that fateful morning in August 1945.

INDEX

Page numbers in **bold** refer to pictures.